Mind
Behavior

By Naomi Hollimon

To order additional copies of this book, contact:
Xlibris LLC
1-888-795-4274
www.Xlibris.com
Orders@Xlibris.com

Abstract

This self help guide will help readers outline the causes and triggers of mental illness. It goes in to depth how to watch for signs that lead to bipolar disorder and the methods of coping with a mental illness once you have been diagnosed. It will leave you with a greater understanding of what bipolar is and the best terms of treatment in getting back to a healthier and more productive lifestyle. As the author you get the in depth scope of this disease from the vantage point of a bipolar for a bipolar. No other guide comes with the angle in which the best understanding and explanation of any written piece is from one who has experienced it firsthand. I hope that you are intrigued to open your awareness and share your new found knowledge on the subject of what it is to be bipolar once you have finished reading.

This is the true self help guide book dedicated to those suffering from bipolar disorder. As the author I share my testimony of a life lived with this disease. The components of this book will help those coping and those dealing with the suffering in many ways. I hope to outline and discuss the impact of the disease and the various ways one can identify the symptoms and manage them as well. There is no rhyme or reason nor is there any magic cure to get rid of those emotions and thoughts that lead to the blind actions systematic of this disease, yet there are methods to help guide you to a more productive and positive life for yourself and those you meet.

Chapter 1
What is bipolar?

To give one definition of what bipolar is would be unfair. The textbook definition will lead you to believe that this disease falls into two categories of a mood or mental disorder, or the combination of both. But is it truly that simple? Bipolars, like myself, can be manic and have the high and low mood disorder. But my experience has led me to believe that a bipolar is a person who had a traumatic life experience. Yes the mania is there and the elevation and downfall of mood is there but more importantly we are living proof that the world and the people in it has a profound impact on us. The disease is caused by that. We don't wake up or are born bipolar. Our disease is the result of a cause that has happened to our minds, bodies and spirits. Everyone is manic or emotionally unstable throughout their lives, so how are some of us bipolar and some of us not? Simple. The average bipolar has that state of being or emotion for a lasting amount of time and is operating or functioning with the aid of medication or therapy to live a semi-normal or productive life. This onset is usually determined by some life altering thing. It could be stress, environmental factors, or other extreme life experiences.

So to define this disease is to say that being bipolar is a state of being that is triggered by trauma to the whole being of a person, causing him or her to think or act in a way outside of their normal and healthy way of who they are. They are forever changed and sometimes reliable on medication or others to grasp the reality of this change and help return them to the state of normalcy they once knew.

Chapter 2
How do you know if your are bipolar?

Like I said before we are all bipolar with our manic thoughts and mood swings.

But this is on occasion for the most part, yet for the chronic sufferer this will be a permanent state of how this person will think or act once diagnosed (or undiagnosed if not treated). For me I knew I was bipolar from the unusual way I was thinking and feeling. After going through a bad break up and other severe personal problems, due to other relationships and stress, my mind and who I was broke. My life was shattered. Who I was, was unknown to me. I could not grasp reality. I didn't know who to trust. Paranoia and fear took over my life. People who I had grown up with and knew all my life became my enemies due to no unforeseen reason. Racing thoughts were now my minds everyday thought pattern. There was no focus or clarity and so I left school on a medical leave and returned to a place and family I distrusted, all to find out that I was now a bipolar.

So to answer the question of how do you know you're bipolar is to say that God gives you from your birth the power of the mind to conceive and think based on reality. He gives you the thoughts that are precise and in order to how you are feeling in a natural and healthy perceived way. When that is changed and you can't even say who and what it is that is real to you any more, then you know. You know this person isn't me. You hear and see things that aren't there. Your feelings and emotions are forever changing from one state to the next. Things that you are sad about are not now in an instance, in which you felt them, but now your life's story. You have to fight for clarity of mind, body and spirit with medicine and therapy. The same things you could of done without that before. So you know your bipolar when the gift of seeing and hearing spirits is no more a gift, but a trauma or a fear in your heart. No one can tell you who you are and who you shall be. But as a bipolar you are different from your Godly created state. Yes you can still function once you are diagnosed as one, but not in the same way in which you are defined by your creator upon when you first took breathe.

Chapter 3
Is medication for me?

This is a hard question to answer and even harder to do if the answer is yes.

I think the solution is relative. If we look at the circumstances that cause a break and find that the problem is stress. Then we see that in stressful situations and triggers that cause stress should be avoided. And to avoid a break caused by increased stress, medicating yourself is usually the answer to avoid such an outcome. The management of the disease is different for everyone. For myself I did have a break due to overwhelming stress put on my mental and emotional state. I also have a family history of the disease which increased my chances of having the break that followed. I did have to be medicated as soon as I had that mental break and maintain that treatment to this day. My dosage has changed and I learn to cope with stress more responsibly, so as not to rely on as much medicine. But the fact is that medication is still needed at this time.

All bipolars, as mentioned, operate differently and are not like me. For some they come out of their break functioning fine, without medication. It all depends on your way of thinking and if your state of mind allows you to function without popping a pill at any given period of time. There are methods to be treated by therapy or other natural remedies that help the suffering bipolar cope daily. The trick is to find out what works for you. If you find that after your initial diagnosis that basing your thoughts on reality and not illusions are your mental makeup then you can, with your doctor, make a plan to avoid taking prescription meds while taking the road back to recovery. But on the other hand if your moods are all over the place and you can't think clearly because your thoughts are manic and of disillusion then the healthy and correct thing to do is to take your medication. Yes there are side effects to meds and you may find it hard to stick to a daily regiment of taking meds, but the benefit does out way the effects. You can't go around not thinking clearly and functioning irrationally in a rationally based world. Until some doctor comes up with a medical cure to rewire the mind and the spirit back to its pre-break days then medication for the bipolar who suffers unclear thinking and emotional disturbance will have to be medicated.

Chapter 4
How do I cope with medication side effects?

Side effects of medicines can sometimes be unbearable and cause the person being treated to stop the medication because of it. These symptoms include everything from dry mouth, weight gain, hair loss, drowsiness, constipation and many more. You ask yourself how am I supposed to get better when this medicine is making me feel worse? And to top it off it is often that these side effects are felt in the body a lot sooner than the healing power of the medicine.

It seems that the antipsychotic or antidepressant is more likely to cause fatigue and weight gain and less likely to help those suicidal thoughts or mania in its initial days of treatment. But again you musn't stop or reduce the dosage because of your current struggle and constant frustration with the process of getting better seeming never ending. Just like the cancer patient who feels worse with getting chemo treatments than he or she does with the actual disease, so to is the battle for many medicated bipolars.

But there are some tricks to eliminating some of the effects of these medications.

For example you can reduce the effects of dry mouth by sipping on ice or drinking plenty of water throughout the day. There are also rinses and mouthwashes that you can purchase to help eliviate some of the effects. To help with hair loss I purchased a hair growth pill and vitamins so to help the process of hair growth and strengthen the hair follicle. It is very difficult to cope with this side effect in particular because the damage can be hard to reverse and effects the appearance and self esteem of the person dealing with it. You may have to switch meds around as well as dosage to come up with the right receipe to treat the symptoms and also manage the effects. I know that research on one's own behalf is key. Doctors who specialize in the field don't always have the time to follow up and keep up with every medications effects on the body and so it is your responsibility to do the educating on medications you are being prescribed. I know that under anti- depressants that Wellbutrin although great with weight loss does cause hair loss and dry mouth. Haldol under anti-psychotics causes weight gain and dry mouth as well. Remember you have to try the medication to see if it works for you and to see if managing the side effects is worth it in comparison to something else.

Yet every medication you take you will have to deal with something, but some are easier to deal with than others. Another thing to consider is generic drugs. These seem to be less potent and less expensive than the brand name medicines in their same category. To treat or help with the side effect of weight gain the most effective thing to do is diet and exercise. I found this very hard to do. Because it has to be a lifestyle change or as long as the medication that is causing the effect is taken. The key thing to remember in any dealing with any disease or situation in which you have to make life changing adjustments is to be determined and hopeful.

Keeping the faith and being diligent to getting better is half the battle won. Whenever you feel like it is over or it's too much to handle just remind yourself it can only get better and the more care you give yourself the better and the sooner those days will come. Support groups, friends and family are motivators that are important for you to keep around you and have in your life. You cannot fight this battle alone and no one is asking you to either. You must rely not only on a team of experts in the medical field to treat your illness but a also a group of believers in the betterment of who you are and can be.

A lot of the healing process for myself is spiritual and my road to recovery is to heal that part of who I am. When I was sick I felt that demons and people who acted in evil ways were after me. And that brought about a paranoia and distrust to everyone around me, even my family. Medication for the longest has been the temporary fix for treating the symptoms, but not the answer. My battle is to complete the struggle from the supernatural to the natural in my mind and spirit. If I can heal what has happened to me spiritually by others and make my mind accept the thoughts associated with it then maybe medication won't be needed. But it is a long road to travel since 2001 and I am still taking the road, twist and turns and all. But I know I am better then I was all those long years ago and will continue to get better with a belief in myself and my recovery. The mind is powerful and the body will eventually heal. The spirit in it also needs direction too, and medication can't cure that. Only you can.

Bipolars need to do soul searching. This disease is not just relevant to the physical but beyond it as well. That is why a lot of sufferers say that they hear voices and see things that are not in the physical. To get better you have to understand the disease and it's process. And in that process you will develop your own source of strength and ways to cope.

Chapter 5
How to deal with a bipolar?

Those who also need help coping with this disease are those suffering along side with the sufferer. I am talking about the family and friends of bipolars. They are also the key to help bipolars back to functioning on the road to recovery. Those who are trained medically in the field of mental health can also use a word of advice in helping treat the ailing. It is key and crucial for those helping take care of the mental ill to recognize the signs and triggers that lead to an episode. These signs before a break and while in an episode will help you prevent and get through this traumatic time. As we earlier mentioned a lot of bipolars go through a series of events or circumstances that lead to their illness. As these stressors occur the mind goes on overload and snaps. Mental, physical and emotional disturbances occur in the body and thoughts and feelings are brought about based on those things experienced. It is those thoughts that need to be dealt with and those emotions that need to be treated. As someone taking care of a bipolar you need to help those suffering work through those lapses. When the imbalance occurs you can medicate, but most importantly helping the person talk it through as well as coming up with coping skills outside of the medicated bottle is crucial.

Many times, if the issue which caused the lapse is dealt with, then the root of the problem is addressed and can be handled accordingly. I know when I got sick I thought that spirits were out to get me and that people were also planning to harm me. Why did I think that way you ask? Simple. It was my thinking developed from the experiences I had. A boyfriend and friends betrayed me and neglected and plotted to harm me. After nowhere to turn and no one to be trusted I opened a Bible, thus entering the spiritual realm of thinking and feeling. With the mental break of not eating and drinking for over three days my mind picked up and acted on dillusions under the stress. I began reading about evil spirits in the Bible and that to protect me I should turn to prayers and Christ.

As I sat in a secluded University dorm room I began my decline in the world of a bipolar. I also began listening to music to feel protected, as my parents and family were across the country being notified of my current condition. I let the lyrics of Bob Marley And Tupac Shakur fill the empty spaces in my room and mind. Luckily my parents found me and brought me back home. Little did they know the endurance and test they would be put under in having to take care of me. This chapter is dedicated in part to their triumph over struggle in taking care of me. My mom especially had to cope a lot more, being my main caretaker. My other family members too had a lot to endure too, to no fault of their own. It would have been easier for someone to give them an exact outline of what to say and do every time I decided not to take my medication or got sick because one didn't work.

Trying to find a happy medium I tried many different ones because I was feed up with side effects. But I now know that all the switching wasn't worth it and that I had to cope and get through my ordeal and help those helping me have an easier go at taking care of me. I remember telling my mother that if I ever got sick for her to tell me that Bob Marley wants me to take my medicine. I said that because in my break that is who I trusted. That is who made me feel safe as I was all alone in that dorm room without my family. The paranoia I felt from feeling people were really demons and people were out to get me was a trigger from the way people were acting around me, forcing me to my seclusion. I say all of this to say that all bipolar have those triggers that will set off an episode and it may be a simple word or gesture that will help those taking care to call them back to reality for a moment in order for you to help them take their medicine or give you a break to get them stable enough to bring them to the hospital. It is up to you as caregivers, family and friends to find out what that is before they have another episode so that you can avoid many more. Let them talk about their feelings and what happened to them to help you determine why they are thinking the way that they are.

Therapy doesn't have to be in a doctor's office but yet a simple conversation in the comfort of their own home. Let the trust begin again with you and people they feel comfortable with. As you develop coping mechanisms then you can think your way out of an episode or treat yourself with less medicine in order to deal with those troubling thoughts and emotions.

The thing to remember is that support is crucial and whether you get it from a family member, friend or doctor you can win your way back to recovery.

Not everyone needs medicine for the rest of your life as a bipolar once they get sick. But if you do, you are not destined to a life of mediocracy or failure.

You can function to a high degree and learn from your experiences. Again keep in mind the spiritual journey too, your life has changed as a bipolar to a higher degree of spiritual and mental thinking. Use that as a gift and testimony to God to help others in your same boat. Learn about your disease and help others become functioning . There are some people who are diagnosed that have not reached that level yet. This is my journey and in writing I hope to not only educate but become a better me. I have learned from my experiences and hope to complete the journey God has in store for me. Like my mom always says, "God made you just the way he wanted you. There are no mistakes or accidents in what God wants for you." You and I are not bipolar because we are a freak of nature or society's outcast. We are bipolar because God wanted us to challenge or mind unlike the rest of the world. And we will know his purpose in searching through this battle and test he has given us. So when we get to the finish line of this race, we are all on, we will know glory.

Chapter 6
Words Never to say to a Bipolar

"Sticks and stones will break my bones. But words will never hurt me." The truth is words do hurt and they have a great impact. This is ever truer for the suffering bipolar or with someone with depression.

Words develop how we think and thus how we act. So choose your words wisely when speaking to anyone, bipolar or not. I know for me to think that I was bipolar when I was first diagnosed was to think that I was "crazy." The thought of someone saying that word or referring to me as that, made me depressed. To say someone is crazy is to say that they don't think clearly and that they are not rationale minded. And though my thoughts were scattered, it was in a moment of stress and pressure on my state of being. My mind, even though fragile, was not going to allow me to act in a way that was going to kill or seriously hurt someone. And for some bipolars that is the case. They, because they do not address their problems, turn into seriously crazed and deranged people. But the thoughts that make up your frame of thinking have to be dealt with. So the power of how you think when you are not manic or depressed have to be coaxed and instilled into who you are. So when those breaking moments occur you rely on what you have stored in you. Like I said before there are trigger words that will break or make any one person if heard over and over again. That is why you should fill your space and mind with positive shows, book, people, thoughts and yes even words. So talk to yourself and tell yourself you are not crazy that those voices are there, but they are not a part of you, and will not dictate how you are going to act. Pick up the phone and call someone when thoughts of suicide or evil warp your brain. Let the positivity of their words put you back on the right path. If you are the person speaking to a bipolar, in a break or otherwise, choose your words to help them see that how they are acting is not how they truly are and remind them of the good person, who would not think or act that way, are. If not for a person find another source of inspiration to guide you out of your downward spiral.

Know who you are and reinforce it every day by what comes into your space and what goes out of it. People who kill their children and others because some voice told them to are, yes sick, but more importantly are acting in a way not true to themselves. Just like out of anger we say or do things that we wouldn't normally. The mind can act in ways that it doesn't normally tend to. But control is what will save you. It is restraint.

Because you know that this is not only right, but not me. Something else is driving me to act. If you can't restrain your actions and or thoughts then know yourself well enough to know what you can't handle and put yourself on medication. You have to live for not only yourself and those around you but God too. And that should be your purpose. That purpose is to find the best part of yourself and share it with others and by doing that you will know that the best part of you is not by being sick or "crazy."

So in conclusion, keep this self-help guide close and your family, friends and Bible even closer. Learn to love and understand yourself and your disease, to help bring about a better understanding of what you are going through. Be diligent and focused on your treatment and it will help guide you to the proper paths and channels to take in order for you to live a productive and fruitful life. God Bless!

www.ingramcontent.com/pod-product-compliance
Lightning Source LLC
Chambersburg PA
CBHW060828290526
45792CB00005BB/1844